DATE DUE		

George and Martha Washington at Home in New York

BEATRICE SIEGEL

ILLUSTRATED BY FRANK ALOISE

FOUR WINDS PRESS

NEW YORK

Special thanks to two historians:

Robert I. Goler for his critical reading of the manuscript and Richard B. Bernstein for lengthy discussions and advice. The contents of the book remain my own.

First Edition   Printed in the United States of America

10   9   8   7   6   5   4   3   2   1

The text of this book is set in 11 point Century Old Style.
The illustrations are rendered in pen-and-ink and watercolor.

Library of Congress Cataloging-in-Publication Data
Siegel, Beatrice. George and Martha Washington at home in New York / Beatrice Siegel; illustrated by Frank Aloise. — 1st ed.   p.   cm. Bibliography: p. Includes index. Summary: Describes the life shared by George and Martha Washington, with an emphasis on the government activities, historical events, and social and sociological aspects of their residence in New York City during the sixteen months when it was the nation's first capital.
ISBN 0-02-782721-6
1. Washington, George, 1732-1799 — Homes and haunts — New York (N.Y.) — Juvenile literature. 2. Washington, Martha, 1731-1802 — Homes and haunts — New York (N.Y.) — Juvenile literature. 3. New York (N.Y.)—History—1775-1865—Juvenile literature. 4. Washington, George, 1732-1799 — Inauguration, 1789 — Juvenile literature. [1. Washington, George, 1732-1799 — Homes and haunts. 2. Washington, Martha, 1731-1802—Homes and haunts. 3. New York (N.Y.) — History — 1775-1865.] I. Aloise, Frank E., ill. II. Title. E312.5.S59 1989   973.4'1'0922 — dc19 [920]   88-24534   CIP   AC

TO MY FRIENDS—
A SUPPORT NETWORK

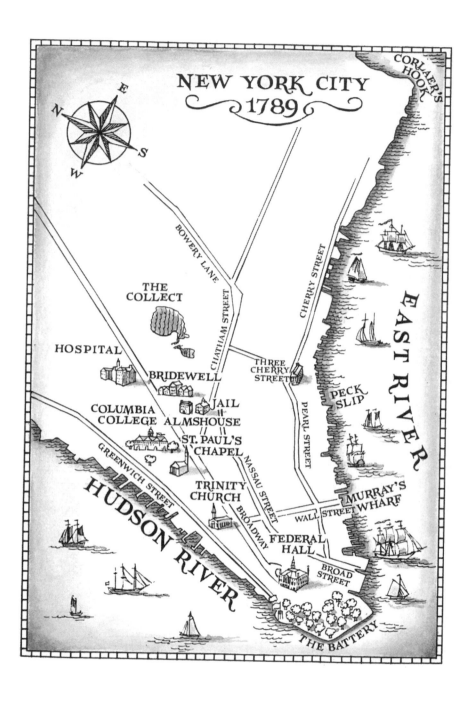

CONTENTS

CHAPTER 1

NEW YORK, NEW YORK

THE NOISE WAS deafening. It rolled and curled around the narrow crooked streets of the seaport town. At dawn the bellowing voices of dockworkers unloading cargo ships had risen up to greet the morning. As the day brightened, the noise seemed to come from everywhere, developing into a discord of jarring sounds: hoofbeats against crudely paved streets, the clatter of carriages and wagons, the wailing clang of hammers. Adding to the turmoil were the impatient voices of shopkeepers renovating storefronts and construction workers repairing buildings. Even street corners were chaotic. Tourists from every part of the country hunched over their luggage, complaining that every bed in every tavern and rooming house was taken. What were they to do? Pitch tents in fields? Nothing, they vowed, would drive them from the city.

Yet over everything lay an air of good cheer, of jubilation. It was April 1789, and New York City, the first federal capital of the nation under the new constitution, was being overhauled for a most unusual event: the inauguration of George Washington, the first president of the United States.

On the corners of Wall and Broad streets, master artisans were putting final touches to Federal Hall. The building, built in 1699 as a city hall, was being enlarged and redecorated to meet the needs of Congress and the president. A French architect had created an imposing structure of Doric columns and arches, of marble floors and painted ceilings. The meeting rooms were hung with crimson draperies and furnished with fine desks and chairs. Marble had been hauled down from New England for the fireplaces.

Even the pediment, the triangular space below the low-pitched roof of the building, was a thing of beauty, decorated with symbols and insignia. Emblazoned on it was a colossal eagle, the king of birds. In one curved claw the eagle grasped thirteen feathered arrows, showing the country's readiness for war; in the other it held an olive branch for peace. Rippling out of the bird's beak was a scroll or ribbon inscribed with the motto *E Pluribus Unum,* Latin for "One from Many" — one country from many states.

Within that one country everyone felt touched by the magic of a new beginning. Only two years before, in 1787, the nation had drafted a new constitution. And here in the heart of a growing seaport city, the experiment in constitutional democracy would get its start. For sixteen months New York City would be the heart of the nation, where rival forces would cradle and shape a government.

The opening chords of the great New York City adventure were struck in 1785 when the Continental Congress moved its headquarters from Trenton, New Jersey, to New York. At once the city sprang to life, putting behind it the dreadful eight years of the revolutionary war, when it had been occupied by the British and became a Tory stronghold. It still wore the scars of that devastation. Churches had been looted and turned into hospitals and prisons. Trees had been cut down for firewood, pavements torn up, and garbage piled high on the streets. Worst of all were the charred ruins glutting the landscape from two fires that had swept through the city in 1776 and 1778.

As if to compensate for that suffering, the news that Congress would make New York its headquarters brought a promise of renewal. It meant a flow of government officials and visitors, a need for housing, shops, food, entertainment, taverns, and inns. It meant jobs and business. As one, the city shed its sorry face and rushed to rebuild, renovate, and repaint. Its first major reconstruction was Federal Hall.

People did not forget the revolutionary war, brought to a close in 1783, only six years before. They held on to an abiding faith in the independence and liberty for which they had fought. And when Congress announced in April 1789 that its electors had unanimously voted George Washington the first president of the United States, everyone went a little wild. Their hero, the commander in chief of the revolutionary army, would be coming to New York to live and to establish among them the seat of the first presidency.

The city buzzed with talk about the overwhelming reception the president-elect was receiving on his journey to New York. City officials, not to be outdone, went into frenzied action to prepare their own triumphant ovation.

Horseback riders, carrying news back and forth, tracked the president from the day he left his home in Mount Vernon, Virginia. At 10 A.M. on April 16 he started north by coach accompanied by an aide, Colonel David Humphreys, and Secretary of Congress Charles Thomson, who had delivered the message of his election.

The crowds and the outpouring of love that greeted him on his journey moved him to tears, for he had not fully realized how popular and beloved a figure he was. Even those who did not support George Washington were nevertheless caught up in the monumental celebration for the first president.

In every hamlet and town people clogged his way. Farmers, artisans, merchants, and workers reached into his carriage to shake his hand, to honor him, to cheer him on.

Horsemen rode out from each town to accompany his carriage. In Philadelphia twenty thousand people lined the streets to watch a cavalry parade salute him. He was feted at a banquet and entertained by a display of fireworks. Arches of evergreen and laurel decorated roads and bridges. In Trenton a chorus of white-clad young women strewed flowers before his carriage and greeted him with an ode. They called him their "defender and protector." "Welcome, mighty chief," they sang.

New York officials claimed Washington from the moment he arrived in Elizabeth Town, New Jersey, and dominated his entry into the city. A congressional committee escorted him onto a specially built barge hung with red satin curtains. Though the barge was equipped with sails, these were disregarded. Instead the privilege of rowing the president across the fifteen miles of

4

the Hudson River fell to thirteen honorary oarsmen dressed in white uniforms and black-fringed white caps.

A burst of cannon fire exploded into the air when the barge reached Staten Island. As if on signal, the Spanish sloop of war, the *Galveston,* anchored in the bay, shot off a thirteen-gun salute at which every vessel in port unfurled its bright colors and flags.

New York City, its businesses shut down for the day, had come to a standstill. The rich and the poor were crowded into the eastern tip of the seaport near Murray's Wharf at the foot of Wall Street. Awaiting George Washington perhaps more eagerly than others in the huge throng were those who had fought with him in the American Revolution. They had been there, alongside General Washington, in the great battles against the British. Most of them were the workers and handicraft people who produced the goods and services for the town, and made up a class of people called mechanics.

They and their families accounted for half the city's population and they were everywhere, the master artisans in elegant shops on Wall Street and the semiskilled and unskilled who worked on the side streets. They were the shoemaker in his small shop and the candlemaker, tailor, and baker next door. They were the masons, tanners, glovers, brewers, and shipwrights.

Having found their voices and power in the war, they were not going to step back into silence. On the contrary, they made their demands known through their trade organizations. They wanted to be able to vote and to have a voice in government. Like all others they venerated George Washington, and they made up the majority of the people waiting for him to arrive.

When the presidential barge finally landed, a thunderous roar of welcome split the air, the church bells rang, the drum and fife corps beat out a steady rhythm.

The president, dressed in simple blue and buff homespun, refused to enter a carriage. Instead, followed by a procession of the town's inhabitants, he walked the short distance to the home provided for him at the corner of Cherry and Pearl streets. All day and evening the celebration went on. Many saw the president enter his carriage in late afternoon for a dinner given by Governor George Clinton.

During the first week after his arrival, Congress was in a turmoil debating how to address the president. Should he be called "His Most Benign Highness," as Vice President John Adams demanded? Or "His Excellency," as others suggested? These titles belonged to a monarchy, many said, not to a democracy. Nor did such titles fit a man as modest as George Washington, a claim made by James Madison, the congressman from Virginia and an old friend of Washington's. Madison's suggestion—to have Washington called simply "the president of the United States"—was approved.

On April 30 when he took the oath of office, George Washington became the president of the United States.

The day started at sunrise with a salvo of shot from the Battery. At 9 A.M. services were held in all the churches. A little after noon, Washington appeared on the small balcony of Federal Hall under the pediment with the swooping bald eagle. Around him were the leaders of Congress. Below him were dense crowds looking up at the man they regarded as a sainted figure. "The savior of our land," the *New York Daily Gazette* called him.

The president was again dressed in an American-made dark brown homespun suit, white stockings, and silver-buckled shoes. His hair was powdered and pulled back in a queue, and at his side hung his plain steel-hilted sword. Only those close to him on the balcony of Federal Hall saw how shaken he was, swearing in a tremulous voice to "faithfully execute the office of President . . . and preserve, protect, and defend the Constitution of the United States." Bending low to kiss the Bible, he murmured, "So help me God."

"Long live George Washington, president of the United States," cried Chancellor Livingston, who had administered the oath. From the huge crowds below the balcony, on rooftops, at windows and doorways, came earsplitting roars, while pealing church bells rolled out over the hilly streets. The president was

grave when he acknowledged the salute from the people. He then walked to the Senate hall to deliver his inaugural address.

In a simple, brief speech, he spoke with veneration of "his" country, introducing a new idea into public consciousness: national pride. And he spoke of the "pursuit of public good."

From Federal Hall, the president led a procession of followers on a short walk to St. Paul's Chapel, where he knelt in prayer. But to return home, he entered his carriage. Those who saw him thought the president appeared a solitary figure amidst the splendor.

Celebrations continued for days, with a display of fireworks and merry crowds filling the streets and taverns. On May 7, the president attended an inaugural ball at the City Arms, an inn on Broadway. The small, fashionable social circle curtsied and bowed in the formalities of a bygone day. The president was comfortable among the distinguished men and women, wigged and powdered, dressed in gleaming satins and brocades. It was reported he had a fine time dancing in two cotillions and a minuet.

Amid all the celebrations, George Washington had one priority: to keep the country united, to hold it together while it took its first steps as a nation.

CHAPTER 2

MARTHA WASHINGTON

MARTHA WASHINGTON MISSED the inaugural ceremony and celebrations. She had remained at home in Mount Vernon to put the house in order and to attend to last-minute packing and shipping of furnishings to New York. But more than practical matters kept her away. She needed additional time to deal with her unhappiness over once again having to disrupt her private life. In her vision of the future, she and the general were to retire forever to the life they loved on the banks of the Potomac River.

At age fifty-seven, after many years of public service, she was asked again to put aside her own needs—this time, to assume the uncertain demands of being the First Lady of the first president of the United States. But never was there any doubt that she would follow the plan laid out for her. She would, of course, travel north to be with George Washington, the country's national hero, and the man she loved and had been married to for over thirty years.

She was born Martha Dandridge on June 21, 1731, in colonial Virginia. Interwoven in her early years was the romance of southern upper-class life: at age fifteen she was a beautiful young woman with dark hair and luminous dark eyes who graced the season's balls in hooped skirt and jeweled headdress. At seventeen she married one of the wealthiest Virginia landowners, Colonel Daniel Parke Custis, a man much older than she. The romance abruptly came to an end less than ten years later when she was widowed and the mother of two young children, Patsy and Jacky. Despite her busy social life and the demands of her large home and lands, she was a lonely woman.

In her were personified the qualities and standards of rich women of her day. She was tutored in reading, writing, spelling, and the social graces: how to walk properly, dance, and curtsy. The skills of household management were included in her education, especially the proper way to supervise the large number of slaves who worked on the plantation and in the home. Under her watchful eye her estate ran smoothly, for added to her abilities were her own affable nature and lively spirit. And like women of her day, she found an outlet for her creative talent in needlework. It was said that her hands were never idle.

The gracious widow Martha Custis met the military hero George Washington in the mid-1750s. The young Washington was an impressive figure, tall and majestic in appearance. At six feet three he towered over the petite five-foot Martha. He seemed to be a silent sort of man, or perhaps he was only shy. Yet he could also be affectionate, as he was with Martha's children.

George Washington, born on February 22, 1732, was a few months younger than Martha Custis. Unlike her he was born into a family of modest means, small landowners who lived on the fringe of wealthy society. His school education stopped in his early teens, but he had the determination and will to learn what he could from books and the people around him. Above all, nature was his teacher, for he had a great love for the outdoors, a sense of harmony with the fields, rivers, and wilderness of Virginia. He grew up near the Potomac River, where he swam as a child, and as a young man, he rode his favorite horse over the fertile land.

At age fifteen he already had a reputation for being fearless and was sent out into frontier land to be a surveyor. At twenty-one he traveled through the Ohio wilderness on a diplomatic mission. And at twenty-two he was made a lieutenant colonel and sent off to fight in the French and Indian War, where he learned the skills of backwoods fighting.

When he turned his attention to politics, he was elected to the Virginia Assembly, called the House of Burgesses, in 1758. There he would meet and mingle with men like Thomas Jefferson, James Madison, and others deeply involved in colonial politics.

By the time George Washington and Martha Custis were married in January 1759, they were both mature people. He was the public figure, sitting in the Assembly in Williamsburg. She brought to the marriage her deep love, enormous wealth, and her two children, creating a warm family life for the reserved man who would never have children of his own.

In the style of wealthy colonists, they decorated their Mount Vernon home and grounds with imported luxuries. Furniture, linens, silver, farm tools, spices for the kitchen, and even children's toys and dolls were shipped across the ocean to the Mount Vernon landing dock on the Potomac. And as part of the elite they indulged in rich entertainments and high living. The social calendar was filled with fancy balls, fox hunting, card playing, and a continuous round of visits. For her travels to friends and family, Martha Washington used a chariot and four horses with a liveried black driver and a postilion, who rode a horse in the leading pair.

Both Washingtons were expert administrators. Martha Washington kept her eye on the household, while George Washington developed his intense interest in farm management and industry. The plantation grew into a self-sufficient complex of thousands of acres stretching ten miles along the Potomac and four miles inland. Atop a steep slope overlooking the river was the house itself, a simple yet elegant mansion.

At the height of its productivity, the plantation housed some three hundred people, most of them black slaves. Martha Washington trained the household help in cooking, sewing, and other domestic chores. Most of the slaves, however, worked on the land, which not only grew tobacco and other crops but was a conglomeration of many businesses. With the help of one or more overseers who lived near the main house, Washington supervised the daily labor of black men, women, and children. They were the ones who planted and harvested the crops, ran the mill, and herded cattle. They were the ditchdiggers and carpenters, tanners, shoemakers, and saddlers. They worked in the fishery business Washington had started on the banks of the Potomac, and they manufactured the linens and woolens in the fabric shop.

Washington was a hard taskmaster, demanding high productivity from his slaves. When they were sick he often thought they were just pretending illness to avoid working. Occasionally when a slave ran away, Washington would pay to have the fugitive recaptured.

If he was intolerant with others, he was equally so with himself, disregarding pain and illness to carry out his many responsibilities. In the company of his overseers, he started the day at dawn, making the rounds on his horse. And just as he diligently kept a journal so did he carefully keep accounts of income and expenditures. He was a skilled administrator, businessman, and farmer. Added to all of these interests was his astute eye in land speculation. He owned 1500 acres in the Shenandoah and thousands of acres in the Ohio Valley.

In the early 1770s, he had an ambitious plan to build a series of canals to connect the Potomac and Ohio rivers, thereby opening up the middle west to settlement. To carry out the project he formed the Potomac Company, of which he was president.

By the time he attended the First Continental Congress in

1774, he was known as one of the wealthiest men in Virginia, physically fearless, disciplined, and daring in warfare. His whole person was commanding and inspired respect. He was tall, yet graceful, with the strong shoulders of an athlete. His face could look impassive, though he had bold features with wideset gray-blue eyes under heavy lids, strong cheekbones, a full mouth, and a protruding nose. His mass of red-brown hair was often tied back in a queue or tail.

When he took his place in the Second Continental Congress in May 1775, fighting had begun at Lexington and Concord. Like many in the gentry, Washington agreed with the radical view that the time had come to talk of independence from England.

No matter what his private ambitions were, he was unprepared for his unanimous election by the Continental Congress to the leading post of commander in chief of a new military force, the American Continental Army. He was concerned more about leaving Martha than about his own inadequacies and wrote to her from Williamsburg about the "uneasiness I know it (the appointment) will cause you," an appointment he regarded as "a trust

too great for my capacity." To his brother, John Augustine Washington, he wrote, "I am embarked on a wide ocean, boundless in its prospect, and from whence, perhaps no safe harbour is to be found."

On accepting his post, Washington announced to Congress that he would accept no salary, only expenses. It was a way of notifying the colonies that he regarded his post as a public service.

At the end of June 1775 Washington took leave of Martha Washington and plantation life and set out for Cambridge, Massachusetts, to lead the armed rebellion against England.

With the first blow for independence, Martha Washington affirmed her place. "My heart is in the cause," she wrote to a friend. Her greatest pain was personal, to see her husband leave on the dangerous and uncertain mission of leading untrained and poorly armed militia against experienced British troops.

Like thousands of colonial women she was filled with pride and patriotism in the call for liberty. She joined the boycott of all imported British goods and foods and convinced her wealthy friends and family to live modestly, to put an end to extravagant entertainment.

When word spread that spinning wheels and looms in every home made a political statement, that colonists would now manufacture their own cloth rather than use Britain's, Martha Washington added sixteen spinning wheels to her home manufacture. She was among the first to wear a dark brown homespun dress.

And like other women, she became a camp follower. Whenever the commander in chief asked her to join him, she traveled in her coach over snow and sleet, across muddy roads and narrow trails, to army headquarters. Loaded into the carriage were food from the Mount Vernon kitchen and the homespun shirts and hand-knitted stockings she and others had worked on over the lonely months.

She was forty-four years old in 1775 when she made the first of many visits to army camps. After a seven-month separation, she set out to visit the general in Cambridge. Accompanied by her son and daughter-in-law, Jacky and Eleanor Custis, and her personal maid, the black woman Oney, she traveled hundreds of miles, arriving in Cambridge on December 11. Immediately she boosted camp morale, entertaining officers and wives in her gracious, hospitable way.

She was a disappointment to those who expected to meet an elegant, slender woman in silk finery, and who called her "Lady Washington." She tried to set a different tone with her simple manner, her dowdy brown dress, and the knitting needles always in her hands.

Among lifelong friends she made in army camp was the lively Mrs. Knox, wife of General Henry Knox, one of Washington's most able aides. Another was Mrs. Mercy Otis Warren, a distinguished author and ardent letter writer who would be called the Pen Woman of the Revolution. In a letter to Abigail Adams, wife of John Adams, Mrs. Warren wrote of dining with Martha Washington and finding her a woman of "ease and cordiality'" and "benevolence of heart," a woman whose "affability, candor, and gentleness qualify her to soften the hours of private life, or to sweeten the cares of the hero."

After the siege of Boston was over, Mrs. Washington joined the general in New York City, where he had gone to build up the city's defenses. What she saw was a tense, grim town surrounded by British ships sailing into the harbor laden with men and ammunition. At the end of June she returned to Mount Vernon bearing countless messages to the overseers from the general. Even in the midst of war he could still think of the problems at home.

Generally Mrs. Washington stayed in Mount Vernon over the spring and summer months and rejoined the general in fall or winter. Sometimes she was housed in elegant homes on her army camp visits; at other times, in cramped quarters. In 1777, after a nine-month separation, she traveled to Morristown, New Jersey, to nurse Washington back to health from a severe illness made worse by his exhaustion. She was with the troops in Trenton, New Jersey, and she was in Valley Forge through the terrible winter of 1777–1778 when thousands lay desperately ill from hunger and fatigue.

Over the years Mrs. Washington became heavyset and full-faced, a small, round figure dressed always in brown domestic fabric, a cap over her graying hair. But her energy and good cheer were enormous, and next to the solemn-faced general, she was always a welcome sight—an inspiration to officers and soldiers and their wives. To everyone she was a symbol of courage, a tireless woman helping to improve conditions in barracks and hospitals. She helped nurse the wounded, and she sat for hours making bandages out of torn-up sheets, petticoats, and tablecloths.

The years brought Martha Washington personal tragedy, the loss of her two children. Her daughter Patsy died at seventeen from a chronic illness, epilepsy. Her son Jacky, who had become a military aide to Washington, died from camp dysentery in November 1781.

CHAPTER 3

THE CALL TO THE PRESIDENCY

FOR GEORGE WASHINGTON, too, the war years brought anguish. Grim military defeats drove him to question his abilities. Surely he meant to say good-bye forever to public life when he bid farewell to his officers of the revolutionary army at Fraunces Tavern in 1783, right after the war.

It was a Thursday, December 4, when George Washington came to the upstairs long room of the tavern and found his men in full military dress. The room blazed with color, the flashing blue, gold, and white of cutaway suits, braided epaulettes, cocked hats and plumes.

Everyone wept openly when he said, "I cannot come to each of you, but shall feel obliged if each of you will come and take me by the hand." Each officer came to him, embraced him, and bade him farewell. After the parting he took a barge across the Hudson River to Paulus Hook and continued on south to Annapolis, where Congress was in session.

He appeared before Congress to resign his commission as

commander in chief of the Continental Army. Again he brought tears to everyone's eyes. Here, of his own free will, was the great patriot-hero declaring that he had no interest in taking over the powers of government, that he was returning it to civilian hands, that he had rejected secret offers to make him a king or a military ruler. He had known that some officers in the army had planned violent actions to establish a royal or a military government. But they needed his support. He made it clear he would not tolerate such treason, such betrayal of the fragile independent country he had fought so hard to gain.

He had only one vision: to return to civilian life. And on Christmas Eve he arrived in Mount Vernon, where only once during eight and a half years had he been able to make a brief visit. He and Martha cherished a passionate dream that they would live out their lives in quiet retirement. He wrote to the Marquis de Lafayette, a young French nobleman who had joined the Continental Army and was almost a son to Washington, that he was free at last to sit "under the shadow of my own vine and my own fig tree."

But George Washington had become a national hero, godlike to the people of the nation. Though he began to relax, riding over the trails of the countryside on one of his favorite chargers, Blueskin or Ajax, his home had become a shrine for hundreds who wanted to shake the hand of the man who led the country to independence. To all visitors the Washingtons were generous hosts, inviting many to stay for dinner. The general enjoyed sharing a bottle of wine with his guests and listening to their jokes and stories.

Both he and Martha were proud of their colonnaded home, within which were gifts of rare bric-a-brac sent by admirers from around the world. The grounds, too, were inspected and admired, for the general enjoyed fussing over his estate. He had put in a circular drive, stables and paddocks, gardens; over all the space wandered goats and sheep and horses. He had planted rare young trees around the driveway, white ash, hemlock, a

21

tulip poplar, and an American holly. He had built a separate apartment for Martha and himself that could be reached only by a private stairway. And he had mounted over the cupola of his home an unusual weather vane, a dove of peace with an olive branch in its mouth.

But it was impossible to be engrossed only in the expansion of his own estate when news reached him daily of problems facing the young nation. The national government had little power. It could not raise money, regulate commerce, or deal with the internal conflicts tearing the country apart. Like the political leaders, he was shocked at the news of the armed uprising in Massachusetts in the fall of 1786. Fifteen hundred small farmers had banded together under the leadership of war veteran Daniel Shays, raided an arsenal, and marched on and set fire to the courthouse. Their paper money was worthless, they could not pay their debts, and they were protesting the foreclosure of their farms. Only six months later could the militia put them down in a bloody skirmish in which several rebels were killed.

Something had to be done to strengthen the federal government, to establish a new set of rules. Washington supported the move to hold a constitutional convention to expand the Articles of Confederation under which the country was governed. Though he headed the Virginia delegation, he did so reluctantly, as if he knew that once he entered Convention Hall in Philadelphia his life would once again undergo radical change. And indeed from that moment his private life was no longer possible, for he was elected president of the convention, a preview of a much greater role.

It was about noon on April 14, 1789, when George Washington opened his door to the horseman who came riding around the circular driveway. Charles Thomson had traveled from New York City to advise him of his election to the presidency of the United States.

Never was a man more reluctant to leave private life. We can begin to understand Washington's feelings through entries in his diary and through letters. We learn how much he wanted to remain in Mount Vernon, to settle into the tranquility of home and family. And we learn the doubts that plagued him, his uncertainty of his popularity, and his reluctance to assume office. Was he suitable for such leadership? he wondered. Did he have the experience and intellectual capacity to deal with complex issues? Could he unify the country, heal the discontent? Could he manage the change from aristocratic values to democratic ones?

He wrote in his diary, "I bade adieu to . . . private life, and to domestic felicity; and with a mind oppressed with more anxious and painful sensations than I have words to express, set out for New York with the best disposition to render service to my country in obedience to its call, but with less hope of answering its expectations."

And he wrote to General Knox that he was "unwilling . . . in the evening of (his) life . . . to quit a peaceful abode for an ocean of difficulties." So unsure was he of his ability to handle high office that he wrote again to General Knox, "My movements to the chair of government will be accompanied by feelings not unlike those of a culprit going to his place of execution."

If so unwilling, why did George Washington undertake the presidency? He was not greedy for power, nor did he have political ambitions. But he did have an unusual spirit of public service, an overwhelming sense of duty to his country. To sacrifice one's personal life was for him an ethical value. The country had summoned him, and he could not say no. He was the soul of the nation, they had said, the popular hero who had the unanimous support of the people. Only he could bind the states together, unify them into one nation.

Martha Washington was different. She did not want to move to New York. Patriotism? In their fifty-seven years she and George Washington had shown their devotion to their country. Now she yearned for the peace and quiet of the Virginia countryside, of the Potomac flowing past her door.

The call to the presidency meant a way of life that had no precedent. She would walk into an unfamiliar world, while the president would take on the anguishing responsibilities of a new government.

Though Washington questioned his popularity on the day of his departure for New York, the answer came swiftly in the outpouring of love on his journey north. And one month later, on May 17, 1789, Martha Washington would learn how popular they both were. From her first days on the road enthusiastic crowds stopped her carriage to greet the First Lady of the land. Her entire journey up north was paved with warmth and joy.

In her carriage with her were her two maids, Molly and Oney, and her two grandchildren, Nelly and Washington Custis. The Washingtons had adopted them after the death of Martha's son, John Custis. Two older children remained at home with their mother, who was about to remarry.

For the Washingtons, the two youngsters helped compensate for the son's loss. Nelly was ten years old and Washington eight when they traveled north with their grandmother. Lively and curious about the excitement around them, they saw their grandmother shake hands with strangers. She was entertained at balls and dinners. In Baltimore a band serenaded her until two A.M., and in Philadelphia church bells rang and the artillery fired a thirteen-gun salute while crowds lining the streets cheered her.

In the rising tide of excitement that met Martha Washington was a new spirit. No longer were the people surrounding her carriage colonists; they were an independent people in an independent country. No longer were there thirteen colonies, each flying its own flag; now one flag spoke for one country under one constitution. And in the liveliness of the people who greeted her were hopes, dreams, and expectations that they would benefit from a free country.

At Elizabeth Town, "Papa," as Martha called the president, was there to meet her. He folded the First Lady in his arms and escorted her to the presidential barge. Along with the children,

maids, aides, and officials, they were rowed across the Hudson by honorary pilots. As the boat sailed up the bay, the cheers of onlookers on the shore reached her, and waiting for them at Peck Slip were the governor, the mayor, and other officials welcoming Martha Washington to New York City.

CHAPTER 4

THE TALK OF THE TOWN

T HE DAY AFTER Martha Washington's arrival, the social elite parked their coaches outside her door and hurried in to welcome the First Lady to town. The presidential house, called the Mansion, was a simple three-story building with five windows facing Cherry Street and another five facing Franklin Square. The rear looked out across the East River to the distant shores of Long Island.

The house had been prepared for the Washingtons by a committee of New York women, among whom were Mrs. Osgood, the former owner of the house, and Lady Kitty Duer. They ran and fetched and carried, seeing to fresh wallpaper and carpeting and selecting the best of silver and dishes. The house was so well appointed that two days after her arrival Martha Washington could hold her first formal reception for New York society.

Never had Cherry Street seen such a flow of carriages and chariots and smartly dressed drivers. The house itself was festive, chandeliers and sconces blazing with candlelight picking up the glistening silken threads on the ladies' gowns. Towering headdresses vied for attention with gay colors and elegant clothes and jewels. Men were dressed in satin or velvet waistcoats and breeches. For the occasion the president wore his favorite black velvet suit with a white vest, shining shoe buckles, his powdered hair tied back in a bag. At his side hung a light dress sword. Martha Washington, holding court, looked splendid in a gown of white and silver brocade. For most of the evening she sat on a straight-backed chair graciously acknowledging the bows and curtsies of her guests. The president, conscious of his role as host, mixed freely with the guests, stopping to chat and smile as he moved among them.

The food served was simple, passed around or set on a large table by servants dressed in red and white livery. Guests could help themselves to plum cake, cookies, candies, tea, coffee, or lemonade. It seemed as if the evening had barely started when word was spread that the president retired early, and at nine P.M. guests began to leave. At ten P.M. the house on Cherry Street was quiet, and the Washingtons had their first reception behind them.

The affair was the talk of the town. Gossips buzzed about the brief evening, that it was hardly regal as befits a president, that the food was skimpy. It was so ordinary, they claimed. Others said the affair was too aristocratic, that it was unseemly for a young republic to imitate a royal court!

For Martha and George Washington official entertainments were, at the least, a hardship, for they sprang from the demands of office and not from friendship. They had to open their home to government people, political visitors, social elitists, and social climbers.

While the Washingtons worked out how best to handle a social calendar, all around them was a ceaseless round of glamorous affairs such as dinners and evening parties. Though invited, the Washingtons felt that it was better not to attend.

Conspicuous among elite hosts were the brilliant lawyer Alexander Hamilton and his wife Elizabeth, daughter of the politically and socially powerful Schuyler family. They gave lavish dinners in their home opposite Federal Hall. In this tight-knit group were also General and Mrs. Knox, and the diplomat and government official John Jay. His wife, the former Sarah Livingston, had lived for years in Spain and France and was among the most sophisticated hosts. The homes of these people glittered with silver and crystal and with the witty talk of illustrious guests, including writers, statesmen, and European dignitaries. On guest lists were the town's affluent bankers, merchants, and

landowners such as the De Lanceys, Livingstons, Clintons, Duanes, and Verplancks. Lady Catherine Duer and Lady Mary Watts attended some of the affairs, adding a touch of aristocracy to the gatherings.

These people made up a small but fashionable and articulate nucleus called the Federal or Republican court. They were the ones invited to the presidential entertainments finally launched by the Washingtons as hosts of the nation.

Friday evenings at 8 P.M. were set aside for Mrs. Washington's receptions. The president, very much at ease at these functions, always made sure that Mrs. Washington was properly acknowledged. Bringing some life to these routine affairs were the grown children of the guests, who added their youthful sparkle to the evenings.

Mrs. Washington's favorite guest was Abigail Adams, wife of Vice President John Adams. Known for her wit and intelligence, she was always seated next to Mrs. Washington, giving the two women an opportunity to talk together. They had much in common, both skilled homemakers and both devoted to their husbands. Though Abigail Adams had a sharp tongue and frankly expressed her hope that women would be included in the new government, she nevertheless played her role as attentive wife to an ambitious and difficult statesman.

George Washington, Mrs. Adams had remarked, was a man made of "majestic fabric." But she also thought highly of Martha Washington and said so in letters to her sister and to her close friend Mercy Otis Warren. In one letter Mrs. Adams described Mrs. Washington as "plain in her dress but that plainness is the best of every art....Her hair is white, her teeth are beautiful...." At another time she wrote that "Mrs. Washington is one of those characters who create love and esteem...an object of veneration and respect."

While Congress was in session another social gathering was added to the Friday evening receptions. Official dinners were held Thursdays at 4 P.M. for members of Congress and their families.

The most ceremonial affair was the levee, an open house on Tuesdays from three to four in the afternoon. On these occasions ritual played a role, for the president had to impress his visitors with the full dignity and authority of his office. He stood stiffly at attention dressed in formal attire, his hat under his arm, a dress sword at his side. The levee catered to the narrowest segment of society. Men only could attend, and only those who were smartly dressed and well mannered. In a way it was a private club for the rich and powerful to be seen in an elite setting, perhaps talking with the president.

In charge of presidential functions was former tavern keeper Sam Fraunces. As the president's steward he supervised the kitchen, its staff, and the purchase of provisions.

In addition to Sam Fraunces was a retinue of servants and slaves that Mrs. Washington had brought with her from Mount Vernon. Among the seven slaves were postilions, grooms, and her personal maids, Oney and Molly. Twelve white servants worked as cooks, launderers, housemaids, and housemen. When necessary, additional staff was hired by the day.

The first year in New York burdened the Washingtons with the need to establish a well-run presidential mansion and a properly balanced social life. They had to satisfy both old-line aristocrats and the general population, who hoped a democratic spirit would flow out of the president's home.

For Martha Washington the first few months were almost painful. She could not tolerate the restrictions placed on her, the dictates of where she might go and what she might do. It deepened her sense of inadequacy, a feeling that she was unequal to lofty official responsibilities. Unlike Abigail Adams and Mercy Warren, she was not a woman of great intellectual attainments. Though she was much loved and respected, these were not happy days for the First Lady, and she expressed her unhappiness in a letter to her niece Fanny Bassett. "I live a dull life here," she wrote, "and know nothing that passes in the town. I never go to any public place. Indeed, I think I am more like a state prisoner than anything else. There are certain bounds set for me which I must not depart from. And, as I cannot do as I like, I am obstinate and stay at home a great deal."

At those times when Mrs. Washington was feeling sorry for herself, she probably sat in an upstairs room of the Cherry Street house. And while she looked out over the East River, perhaps in her mind she fancied herself in Mount Vernon with the Potomac flowing by. That was where she yearned to be.

Though she would refer to the first months as "lost days," she was not always gloomy and despairing. Too many responsibilities claimed her, among them the care of her grandchildren. She supervised them carefully, demanding that Nelly Custis practice the spinet she had shipped from Mount Vernon, later replaced by one of the pianos made by a New York craftsman. No matter how much Nelly protested, she had to take three music lessons a week. She was also enrolled as a day student at the fashionable Mrs. Graham's School, newly opened on lower Broadway. Washington Custis, not so easy to manage, was instructed at home by private tutors.

31

New York's small theater, located on John Street off Broadway, offered both Washingtons real pleasure. Here was a form of entertainment that even the children were brought to by the president's secretary, Tobias Lear. Washington, always an ardent theatergoer, had attended plays while in Williamsburg, and in New York had gone to a play within two weeks after his arrival. Accompanied by John Adams and other government officials, he had seen Sheridan's *The School for Scandal* and a popular comic opera called *The Poor Soldier.* To please the president, a box decorated with the government seal was set aside for him and the family. And here Martha Washington acknowledged the greetings of the audience when she entered the president's box.

The official schedule had hardly gotten under way when it was interrupted. In mid-June Washington complained of feeling feverish. Doctors discovered he had a tumor deeply imbedded in his thigh and ordered immediate surgery. After the painful operation, he was confined to bed for weeks of rest.

Martha Washington took over care of the sickroom and saw to it that the patient had complete quiet. She had a rope stretched in front of the house to prevent vehicles from drawing up, and she had straw laid down on the streets to silence the clatter of horses and iron-wheeled carriages.

As soon as he was pronounced out of danger, the president became restless, eager to be out and around. The first thing the Washingtons did was to remodel their coach so that the president could stretch out fully on his side for rides around the city. By mid-October, his health fully restored and Congress adjourned, he set out for a tour of New England. It was exactly the stimulation he needed, to visit farms and factories. More than anything, his spirits revived from the show of enormous popular support. Towns were festive, dinners and fireworks awaited him, crowds surrounded his carriage.

George Washington's popularity was summed up in Boston, where an arch and colonnade built especially for him was inscribed with the words: To the Man Who Unites All Hearts.

CHAPTER 5

"THE FOURTEEN MILES ROUND"

NOT EVEN THE intense pressures of office could force the president to be physically inactive. He was too energetic and restless, and the need for exercise frequently took him outdoors. In the company of Tobias Lear, he would walk along the Battery, where he could look out over the harbor, or stroll along Wall Street, the fashionable promenade.

Horseback riding was a necessity for the president, and whenever possible, he rode his horse into the space and freedom of the countryside. Among his pleasures was an exercise with the family, a leisurely ride in a coach and four with Mrs. Washington and the children. He would call these family excursions into the rural areas "the fourteen miles round."

He had become fond of Manhattan Island. Especially appealing was the way it lay between two broad rivers, the swift-flowing East River on one side and the Hudson on the other. It encompassed some twenty-two square miles extending northward from the Battery. The town itself did not extend the full length

of the island. On the east side, it covered one and a half miles to Bayard's Lane (now Broome Street), and on the west it extended one mile to Reade Street. Along both waterfronts were large, busy markets for fresh produce, and dotting streets and alleys were taverns and shops.

Despite its natural beauty, the city was in a continuous upheaval of expansion and change. Hills were being leveled, valleys filled in, and sidewalks widened, giving the city a new look. Additional streets were being created by landfill along the waterfront, which was a mess of noise and excavation.

But business went on as usual, and the harbor was filled with sailing vessels carrying on the country's booming foreign trade. Just a few years before, amid great celebration, the first American ship, the *Empress of China,* was sent off on the first round-trip to the fabled land of Asia. Brisk business on land and sea brought a spurt in the city's population. By 1790, in the first federal census, it was over 33,131, making New York second in size only to Philadelphia.

Not all of New York's citizens were engaged in commerce. Away from the business centers, the city was rural. Much of the area covered in the Washington family's long drives was countryside.

For these excursions, the family chose a simple coach and four horses, for only a small carriage could navigate the narrow winding lanes often blocked by water carts, butchers' wagons, and pigs freely roaming over the streets.

From home the carriage traveled along the east side onto Bowery Lane going north. On the way it passed the "Jews' Burial Ground," and a bit north of it was the beginning of farmland and the famous twenty-two-acre farm (south of present-day Union Square) belonging to the Baron Poelnitz. The president, a farmer at heart, usually stopped here whether on horseback or in the carriage. The Baron was experimenting with crops, fruit trees, and machinery, trying out a different type of hoe and plow. And like the president when he was at Mount Vernon, the Baron was something of an inventor, making new gadgets for his farm implements.

Continuing north on Kingsbridge Road, the carriage would pass old mansions such as the Kip house; built in 1655, it was one of the oldest in the town. Further on was the famous Beekman mansion (near present-day First Avenue and Fiftieth Street), and on the carriage went, over small bridges — one of them called a kissing bridge — on up to McGowan's Pass (present-day 108th Street). Then west along a Harlem lane until

the carriage reached the Bloomingdale region on the Hudson River (about 94th Street), when it turned south down the west side toward home.

On the long, tiring drive, the Washingtons would stop at an inn for cakes and tea. Or they would call on John and Abigail Adams, whose home, called Richmond Hill, was built on several acres of land. The beauty of the place often sent Mrs. Adams into rhapsodies of praise. In a letter to her sister she described in detail the house on a hundred-foot hill overlooking gardens, fields, shrubbery, and the wide Hudson with its "majestic waves, bearing upon his bosom innumerable small vessels." The pastures were "full of cattle," she wrote, and "a lovely variety of birds serenade me morning and evening, rejoicing in their liberty and security." In natural beauty, she said, her house and grounds could vie with the "most delicious spot" she ever saw.

After the visit, the Washingtons continued down the west side toward home. Describing the excursion, the president wrote in his notebook that he "exercised with Mrs. Washington and the children in the coach between breakfast and dinner . . . in the fourteen miles round."

On his rides and walks around the city, the president explored it thoroughly. He had to notice that there were two parts to it, the beautiful and the wretched. For even in 1789 New York City had its very rich and its very poor.

As the seat of federal, state, and local governments, the city attracted politicians, the wealthy, the fashionable, and the cultured. Adding to the city's prestige were the distinguished men in Congress carrying out the mandates of the new constitution. Many of them, caught in the housing shortage, boarded at the elegant Mrs. Daubenay's on Wall Street, or in Huck's Tavern on Williams.

The president and Mrs. Washington felt comfortable among these privileged people who gave the city its social standing. Their close friends were in this class. Though they made up only a minority of the population, they were powerful and articulate, their comings-and-goings filling newspaper columns.

The poor, on the other hand, were mostly invisible, tucked away in the outer wards of the fashionable metropolis. On his rides around the city the president saw the run-down houses, and he caught glimpses of the homeless sleeping in doorways or beggars wandering the streets. That inequality existed was not surprising; only the extent of it was. There were thousands of poor, among them black and white, old and young. And not far from Washington's home on Cherry Street were the city's worst slums.

CHAPTER 6

THE OTHER CITY

I F THE PRESIDENT stepped out of his house and walked north, he would come to Corlaer's Hook, a spit of land that curved around the East River. There he would find the newly relocated shipyards, where business was beginning to expand and where the waterfront was becoming a sailors' haven of cheap taverns and boardinghouses. The narrow unpaved streets that led to the shipyards were muddy from the overflow of the marshland along the banks of the river. Yet on these lanes stood the run-down wooden houses that were homes to the poor and jobless. No amount of housekeeping could brighten these shabby shelters, where families shared small rooms and slept on beds made of straw spread over damp floors.

The slum extended down around Rutgers Yard into Bancker, Oliver, and Catherine streets. Here, black people, isolated by both race and poverty, had settled.

If the president wanted to explore other mean streets, he could turn south after leaving Cherry Street. At the end of the

East River, not far from where his barge had landed, was Canvas town, called that because the homeless had built shelters of canvas there after the war. Now the town's residents were advised to stay away from the area; it was dangerous, a place for "dissolute characters."

As the number of poor increased, they took over more neighborhoods, and upper Broadway near the freshwater pond called the Collect became an area of shoddy housing. The Collect and its offshoot, the Small Collect, were fed by deep springs that had been the major source of fresh water for the Indians and early European settlers. By 1789 the water from the Collect was considered a health hazard. Deep wells supplied the town with water through the "Tea-water pumps" on Chatham Street. Cartmen, a boisterous lot dressed in long white frock coats over their trousers, lined up to load their wagons with barrels of water, which they sold to homes and public buildings by the gallon.

By the time the Washingtons settled in New York, they could learn only through stories of the good old days when the ponds were used for fishing in summers and ice-skating in winters. Those were the days when the hundred-foot hill around the Collect became an arena for spectators watching the winter sport.

Businesses took over the land around the ponds. Tanneries spread their rows of vats for the processing of leather, polluting the air with an awful stench. Here too potteries, breweries, starch and glue factories, sail and rope shops, and other trades that drew water from the Collect were established. In and around the factories, on patches of dry land above the marshes and bogs, were homes for semiskilled workers like the cartmen and for others who needed low-income housing.

The days of the freshwater ponds were coming to an end. They had become polluted water holes filled with industrial and human wastes, and in 1790 there was talk of using the earth from the surrounding hills to fill them in, creating flat usable land in the process. In general the city had inadequate health supervision. When epidemics occurred, such as yellow fever, the impact was enormous, especially among the poor.

Nowhere was the city a picture of sharper contrasts than in the neighborhood south of the Collect. On the streets between Columbia College and St. Paul's Chapel, where the president and his family worshiped, were large, elegant homes. Opposite them was a park, or commons, as it was called. At the northern end of the commons were huge, ominous-looking buildings that mirrored the lives of the poor. Standing near each other were the Bridewell prison, the Almshouse, and a debtors' jail.

What could be a sorrier sight than the Almshouse filled to capacity with abandoned children and infants and with the crippled, blind, aged, and sick? The Almshouse sheltered and clothed them and, in later years, created work projects for the physically able.

In the vicinity of these buildings were grisly sights. One was the gallows, gaudily painted to look like a Chinese pagoda to veil its cruel purpose. In 1789 ten people were put to death for nothing more serious than burglary. Near the gallows were the stocks and the whipping post, where the public whipper lashed offenders on their bare backs.

The nature of punishment reflected the moral attitude toward poverty and petty crime. These social ills developed, the popular belief went, not from social or economic conditions, but from some weakness within people, from ineptness and ignorance; or they were natural to a person's station in life. It was thought that workers, for example, received low wages and barely survived because it was normal for their class to live that way. These ideas also prevailed in other cities of the thirteen states, for conditions for New York's poor paralleled those in other growing urban centers.

This general attitude might account for the president's comments during his New England tour when he visited a factory and observed women and children working at textile looms. He accepted it as natural that they worked a ten-hour day, from eight in the morning to six in the evening. He commented that it was an improvement over farm life. He never thought, nor did his contemporaries, that the fate of the textile workers could be different, or that children should not work at all.

Though the poor were numerous in New York City, it was hard to pin them down. They moved from place to place looking for work, and often city directories did not list them. They became people without names and addresses, people with hidden histories. Their most serious condition sprang from their powerlessness, for according to the rules of the day they could not vote. Suffrage was limited to white males who owned property or paid taxes. These voting requirements eliminated the propertyless, as well as all women, blacks, and Indians. Since these segments of the population had no voice in government, no one spoke up for them.

None had a greater sense of dignity than the revolutionary war veterans. Here were people who had made up the militia and the armies. Many had been wounded or were suffering from the traumas of war. They had returned to New York to find the city in ruins, their homes destroyed, their jobs gone. Like all people in the poor parts of town, they needed help. And like all people, they turned to the president, known for his loyalty to his soldiers.

Though poverty had gotten a toehold in the city, neither the president nor other political leaders discussed the issue. It was not, at that time, considered a matter for government responsibility. Only after many years of struggle would systematic procedures be developed for social welfare. In Washington's day poor relief was random and uncertain.

One popular method of helping the poor was through the charity of the wealthy who made special gifts at holidays. Though the president tried to keep his benevolence secret, it leaked out that on Thanksgiving of 1789 he had made an "acceptable donation" to the inmates of the debtors' prison.

Welfare sometimes got a boost through special city legislation when funds were made available to the poor in their homes. They would be supplied with food coupons, firewood, an occasional holiday meal, and sometimes with work relief. The church was a major source of support through its overseers, who allocated funds for needy parishioners. The mechanics, too, began

to take care of their own, organizing mutual aid societies in the trades.

These bits and pieces of poor relief were only temporary solutions. Something had to be done, because the poor were a source of worry. They had a history of unpredictable violence, when the power of their numbers rocked the nation. No leader could forget the Daniel Shays armed uprising of 1786, when powerful men trembled at what they saw as threats to a weak government. The event had pushed George Washington and other leaders to create a constitution providing for a strong central government, one that could meet dangers not only from abroad but also from within the country.

But violent actions continued to occur. The causes for them varied, but the fact that crowds of people could band together and take matters into their own hands remained a challenge to political leaders. One such "mob" action took place in New York in April 1788, one year before George Washington took his oath of office. It was known as the "Doctors' Riot."

It started innocently, when a foolish medical student studying

at the hospital dangled the arm of a corpse from an upper window to dry. It caught the attention of some boys playing on the grounds below. One of the boys, who had just lost his mother, rushed home to report the incident to his father, a mason. The mason aroused his neighbors, who had known for some time that medical students had been dragging bodies out of the potters' field, the Negro burial ground, and other cemeteries. They were desecrating graves to use the bodies for dissection.

Enraged by the students' insensitivity, the mason, his friends, and a large crowd of neighbors armed themselves with whatever was at hand: tools, knives, staves, crowbars, hammers, stones. They surrounded the hospital, broke open the doors, and destroyed anatomy specimens in the medical cabinets. They dragged medical students from their hiding places and handed them over to the police, who put them in jail, pending a trial. Even the police shared the outrage at the desecration of burial plots.

The next day the violence grew worse when protesters searched physicians' homes for bodies, then stormed the jail, broke windows, tore down fences, and threatened to kill every doctor in the city.

A ten-year-old boy, William Alexander Duer, was watching the violence from the window of his home opposite St. Paul's Chapel. To him it looked like "civil war in the street." The city was "in a state of siege," as he described it years later in his memoirs.

He saw a threatening crowd gather at the entrance of the commons, hurling stones at troops called out to quiet them. Prominent political leaders were called on by the governor and mayor to help restore order. John Jay, while addressing the crowd, was wounded in the head by stones, and the revolutionary war general, Baron von Steuben, was knocked down. To William Duer's great excitement, both were carried into his home, where his mother treated their bloody wounds.

The protest was finally put down by the armed militia, which fired into the crowd, killing three and wounding many others.

A mason led this attack, rounding up other mechanics or artisans for the protest. For the mechanics, as a class, ranged over the city like an arc connecting poor and rich. At one end of the spectrum were the unskilled and semiskilled workers who barely survived on low wages and seasonal employment. Sickness or economic depression threw them right in among the very poor. At the other end of the spectrum were the master craftsmen, a few of whom were stepping up into the merchant class.

United by common needs and expectations, the mechanics were powerful and articulate. They showed their pride in their work through craft organizations, each of which had its own banner and slogan. In a parade or rally, the Society of Pewterers, for example, would raise high its painted silk banner inscribed with the slogan Solid and Pure. The umbrella organization of the trades, the General Society of Mechanics and Tradesmen of New York City, proudly displayed a banner showing a muscular arm and a clenched fist holding high a hammer.

In local elections, where many could vote, they put up their own candidates, "men of their own class," was how they put it.

They were getting a foot into the political doorway, hoping to loosen the city from upper-class domination.

The elite continued to speak disdainfully of the mechanics, calling them "base," "inferior," and "mean." These lower-class common folk should be happy, went the talk, to be guided by the rich educated ones at the top of the social scale.

But such concepts no longer affected the mechanics. For them, the American Revolution had been a dividing point, giving them a new way of thinking. Above all the revolution gave them a sense of their strength, and they would use it to gain their rights.

They knew that George Washington was true to his class, that he had his place among influential merchants and financiers. He shared with them the idea that wealth and class interest gave the rich a special stake in the government.

Though Washington's beliefs were contrary to the demands of the mechanics and others who wanted a voice in government, he nevertheless remained a beloved figure. There was a popular image of George Washington that made him the idol of the poor as well as the rich.

He lived simply and had a reputation for thrift and industry. He was honest, disciplined, and completely lacking in personal ambition and that greed for power that could threaten the country. The men who fought alongside him against the British remembered the general who was tireless, caring, a man of incredible physical courage. In the popular mind, he had the common touch: here was a man, they thought, who could step outside of his class and be one with them.

The president, in need of a united country, depended on the support from all the parts of the nation's population. Facing him were critical issues, ones that could divide the country. One such issue was slavery.

CHAPTER 7

SLAVES AND SERVANTS

WHEN GEORGE AND MARTHA WASHINGTON came to live at 3 Cherry Street, New York City was the center of the antislavery movement. As the seat of the federal capital the town seethed with the passions of black people and the local and national abolitionists who wanted to put an end to a hateful institution.

But both Washingtons were products of a slave society. They were born and raised in the South, into a way of life that flourished on a plantation economy and slave labor. George Washington had inherited slaves from his own family and on his marriage to Martha Custis had become the owner of her slave population as well. And as they bought more land, they bought more slaves. They had always moved comfortably within that culture and perhaps even thought that slavery was a natural way of life. In the North, however, where slavery did not play as vital a role in the economy, they would be exposed to different experiences and points of view.

49

In the years before the American Revolution, a growing community of people wanted to see slavery abolished. Slave auctions, as symbols of hideous inhumanity, were among the first things to be attacked. In New York the slave market built in 1709 at the foot of Wall Street began to fall into disrepute when newspapers joined in the abolition fight. The *Long Island Herald* called slave auctions "disgraceful to humanity."

By the 1770s the question of slavery was an urgent topic throughout the Northeast. But every gain was contested, and New York City reflected the contradictions of the time. On the one hand, it offered sanctuary to fugitive slaves; on the other, it was legally obligated to return such slaves to their masters.

Abigail Adams, in a letter to her husband in 1774, expressed one popular northern attitude toward slavery. "I wish most sincerely there was not a slave in the province," she wrote; "it always appeared to me a most iniquitous scheme to fight ourselves for what we are daily robbing and plundering from those who have as good a right to freedom as we have. You know my mind upon the subject."

But it took the American Revolution to strike the first serious blow against slavery and to introduce George Washington to different attitudes. The revolution made a new vocabulary popular — words like *freedom*, *liberty*, and *justice*. "All men are created equal," said the Declaration of Independence. All men? Are we not men? black people asked.

More than words undermined the institution of slavery. During the revolution the British launched an aggressive policy to weaken colonial strength by disrupting slave status. They wooed the slaves and urged them to flee from their masters, offering them shelter and freedom if they enlisted with the British. The tactic was so successful that it forced General George Washington to reconsider the policies of the Continental Army excluding all blacks from service. At the close of 1775 and in early 1776, Washington appeared before Congress to urge that free blacks be permitted to serve in the American army. It was essential, he said, to prevent them from fighting with the British.

New York State, encouraging blacks to enlist, promised slaves full freedom after three years of military service. And to win compliance from farm slaveholders, the state offered five hundred acres of public land for each slave permitted to volunteer. As a result of such policies, five thousand blacks fought alongside white soldiers in the Continental Army, and many were in local militias.

The Revolution not only made liberation possible for many blacks, but it also gave freedom to thousands of indentured servants. Many of these entered the army, weakening the system of importing bonded servants from abroad.

British disruption continued to the very conclusion of the war. In 1783 when British ships sailed away, they had on board not only ten thousand colonists but also more than three thousand blacks who, on reaching England, Canada, and the West Indies, entered the general population. Thousands of others, inspired by slogans of equality, deserted plantations and artisan shops. They moved into northern towns where slavery was prohibited, such as Boston, or fled to Canada, or settled among the Indians.

Antislavery feelings ran high in New York City, where free blacks spoke up and the fight for manumission, or emancipation, was led by the Quakers. This religious group was strong, vocal, and uncompromising in proclaiming that slavery was incompatible with the ideology of the American Revolution and the concept of freedom for all. The New York State Legislature had adopted a resolution that said the time had come when "every human being who breathes the air of this State, shall enjoy the privileges of a freeman."

All forms of slavery came under attack, and in 1784 a group of New Yorkers raised money to free a cargo of indentured servants newly arrived from Europe.

By 1785 many organizations were advocating emancipation. The leading group, the New York Society for Promoting the Manumission of Slaves, was headed by Washington's friend, John Jay. Among other members were prominent citizens such as Alexander Hamilton, James Duane, and Chancellor Livingston.

These groups succeeded in getting legislation passed that weakened slave traffic. A 1785 law prohibited the import of slaves into New York. By then the public outcry was fierce, the press joining in the attack on slavery. The February 4, 1785, issue of the *New York Gazeteer* called the trade "cruel, wicked, and diabolical."

Antislavery work in New York created new possibilities for black people. In 1787 the first school for black children opened its doors. The twelve initial students grew to fifty-six one year later.

Though the 1780s saw a serious crippling of slave institutions, there were always loopholes, and the sale of slaves continued. On April 7, 1789, the *Daily Advertiser* carried this item: "TO BE SOLD A Negro Fellow aged twenty . . . expert at waiting and every kind of house-work." Another item announced, "FOR SALE A young Negro girl twelve years of age, strong and healthy, bred in the country, and used to the business of a farm."

On that day the same newspaper carried a headline that overshadowed both these advertisements. It announced that the United States Congress had counted the ballots of electors and had unanimously elected George Washington president.

In 1789 black people made up about ten percent of the city's population. Of them 1,101 were free blacks and 2,369 were slaves. They did the household work in large city homes or they were put to work as laborers in artisan shops. Many became skilled tailors, bakers, tanners, blacksmiths, masons, and butchers. But by class and race, the free blacks were isolated into the poorer sections of town.

When the Washingtons moved into this feverish antislave climate in 1789, they brought from Mount Vernon seven of their favorite slaves. Mrs. Washington never traveled without one or both of her two personal maids, Oney Judge and Molly. The women were trained as seamstresses by Mrs. Washington and instructed in caring for her personal needs. Among the other slaves were the president's valet, Bill, and grooms and postilions.

But the president had received a liberal education up north in his leadership of an interracial army, and he was aware of all the antislavery agitation that followed the Revolution. He was in painful conflict over his ownership of slaves and had begun to abhor the institution. As early as September 1786, he had written to John F. Mercer, the political leader in Maryland, "I never

mean, unless some particular circumstance should compel me to it, to possess another slave by purchase."

As president of the country, he not only had to solve his personal conflict but also to forge unity out of the pro-slavery and antislavery factions in government. For at the second session of Congress, convened in January 1790, slavery was an explosive issue.

The Quakers and other abolitionists were demanding that Congress pass antislavery legislation. At the top of their agenda was a measure that opposed the outfitting of a ship in New York Harbor that would sail to Africa to bring back slaves. The legislature said it could not interfere. In the heated debate on the issue, Representative Thomas Scott of Pennsylvania said, "I look upon the slave trade to be one of the most abominable things on earth; and if there was neither God nor devil, I should oppose it upon the principles of humanity and the law of nature."

Much as slavery troubled him, the president could not make a forthright statement in favor of immediate abolition. He could foresee that the issue, unless solved, would split the country in two. He made clear that he favored an orderly legal procedure for emancipation, and criticized the Quakers and others whose tactics, he said, were divisive.

Still, he was uneasy. The depths of his feelings became known after his death, when his will was read. In it, he stipulated that the hundreds of slaves on his Virginia plantation were to be freed upon the death of Martha Washington, and that provisions were to be made for the care of the aged and for the education of the young. Martha Washington did not wait for her death to free the slaves. One year after George Washington's death in 1799 and before hers, she arranged for the freedom of the slaves at Mount Vernon.

CHAPTER 8

"I Walk on Untrodden Ground"

NEVER DID THE president forget that his goal in office was to get a weak nation started on a steady course. To do so, he had to unite all opposing voices. Only an orderly, strong government, he said, could move the country forward.

Aware of the pitfalls surrounding him, he wrote to a friend during the first months of his administration that few "can realize the difficult and delicate part which a man in my situation had to act . . . my station is new; and, if I may use the expression, I walk on untrodden ground."

The first session of Congress had to consider practical matters, among them raising money to run the country, honoring its war debts, and providing a national currency.

Nevertheless Congress found time to enact far-reaching legislation such as the Judiciary Act, which gave the country a system of federal courts. Even more significant for the welfare of the nation was its unanimous approval of the first amendments to the Constitution, which have become known as the Bill of Rights.

These first amendments reached out into the hearts and minds of every individual. They put to rest fears that the new federal government would cater only to the needs of the privileged, usurp state power, and ignore the personal rights and freedoms of the general public. These fears had led to fierce debates among the delegates to the Constitutional Convention in Philadelphia in 1787. Only with the assurance that individual rights would be protected did the Virginia and New York legislatures agree to support ratification of the new constitution.

In the spirit of that promise, Congressman James Madison of Virginia presented the amendments at the first session of Congress and urged their speedy approval and ratification. President Washington was known to support the amendments, and indeed their passage helped provide the stability he needed during the first perilous months of government.

The Bill of Rights did two things: it limited the powers of the central government in relationship to individuals and to the states. It further stated that all powers not given to the federal government would be undertaken by the states. It also guaranteed basic rights, among them freedom of the press and of religion, speech, and assembly; trial by jury; and protection against illegal entry and search of homes.

The president, always aware of his shortcomings when dealing with the complexities of government, did not hesitate to consult those whose experience and knowledge he respected. To head four newly created government departments, Washington chose men who would later be called the cabinet. He made General Knox secretary of war, Alexander Hamilton secretary of the treasury, Thomas Jefferson secretary of state, and Edmund Randolph attorney general.

The president expected harmony among his close aides. But in Alexander Hamilton and Thomas Jefferson, he had two brilliant men with radically different visions of the country's future. Their opposing views would set in motion the very divisiveness that Washington dreaded.

Alexander Hamilton, born in the West Indies and educated at King's (now Columbia) College, had proved his courage and bright mind during the Revolution as a trusted aide to Washington. Upon his marriage to the wealthy daughter of one of the leading New York families, he became socially and politically prominent. Schooled in law, he was able, aggressive, and outspoken about the need for a powerful central government. He became a leader of the Federalists, a group that had the president's support and that included wealthy merchants, landholders, and bankers. They believed that only a strong government could lead the country toward economic growth; only such a government could prevent chaos by controlling the unpredictable actions of the unprivileged.

According to the Federalists, common people could easily be led astray and, in general, they lacked the qualities for self-government; the upper class, however, with its large financial interests in government, could give it stability.

Thomas Jefferson was opposed to these views. Though born into great wealth, he nevertheless had faith in the abilities of common people to govern themselves. He feared strong central government and the corrupting power of privilege.

Jefferson, a Virginian, was like Washington a large plantation owner and knew the president from their years together in the House of Burgesses. Though he respected Washington's courage and leadership, he nevertheless became the leader of the anti-Federalists, those who favored strong state governments and a decentralized federal government.

In Jefferson's vision of America, there would be space for everyone to work, own homes, and live comfortably. He saw the country as a rural idyll where lilacs bloomed in barnyards and farmers moved into the wilderness to create peaceful communities. He loathed the idea of busy commercial cities with pockets of poverty that denied human values.

Hamilton and Jefferson, both powerful advocates of their beliefs, led completely opposite factions. These factions would hinder the efforts toward unity that Washington craved and provide the groundwork for a future two-party system.

Thomas Jefferson did not take over his office until March 1790, long after the first session of Congress had adjourned on

September 29, 1789. That session was memorable for its unity and quiet.

When Congress reconvened in January 1790, Washington's personal popularity remained high. But bitter debates, among them arguments about the emotional issue of slavery, would set the country on a new course.

In his first Annual Address, the president itemized vital issues before the country such as organization of a militia and an army, and other matters of defense. He also recommended a uniform system of weights and measures, and better roads and post offices. But the topic that touched him most was education and its role in building a just society.

George Washington, largely self-taught, had the highest respect for learned men and women. He urged Congress to enact legislation that would introduce a broad system of education, provide money for seminaries, and perhaps establish a national university. Only an informed people, he said, could guard their constitutional rights and judge whether they were being unjustly oppressed.

Washington spoke about education and other issues that he

felt deeply about, but the heart of the congressional session belonged to Alexander Hamilton and his report on the state of the treasury. Hamilton proposed that the federal government not only pay back the large national debt of some fifty million dollars accumulated during the Revolution, but that it also assume the burden of paying back the debts piled up by state governments.

These debts were in the form of bonds, and he proposed to redeem them at face value. The bonds, however, had fallen in value after the war and though considered worthless, had been snatched up by shrewd speculators at a fraction of face value. If the government redeemed the bonds at face value, it would enrich the speculators and not the war veterans and small farmers who had originally purchased them.

Bitter and passionate debate raged in Congress over Hamilton's proposals. James Madison put up a valiant fight to have the original owners of the bonds, who desperately needed money, paid back at least in part. But his proposals were defeated.

Walking into the midst of the angry controversy was Thomas Jefferson, who arrived from Europe in March 1790 to assume office as secretary of state. In long discussions with Hamilton

and others, a compromise was reached. It did not benefit the war veterans at all, but it did calm a regional conflict that was also raging.

The agricultural southern states had already paid off their war debts, so they would not profit from the bond payments. They argued that Hamilton's plans benefited northern bankers and landowners, and that the site of government in a northern city also strengthened these interests. They wanted the federal government moved south, where they could exercise some control.

In the compromise reached, the federal government assumed all debts. In return for winning on this issue, Hamilton and his supporters agreed that the government would move to Philadelphia for ten years while a permanent capital was built along a ten-mile stretch of land bordering the Potomac River. The South accepted this plan; the bankers and speculators were enriched; and the fate of New York City was decided—it lost its status as the country's capital.

CHAPTER 9

FAREWELL

IN THE MIDST OF all the debate in Congress, the Washingtons moved to larger quarters. They took over the McComb house on lower Broadway between Trinity Church and the Bowling Green. Surrounded by gardens and a view of the Hudson and the New Jersey shoreline, the spacious house and grounds were more appropriate to their position than the Cherry Street house. The president had personally overseen the preparation of the stables to make sure his sixteen horses would be comfortably cared for. His love for them dated from his Virginia childhood, and fine horses, saddle equipment, and carriages were essential to his way of life.

And the Washingtons put on a dazzling show when they attended state or festive events. To the excitement of onlookers, they were driven through the streets in their gilded chariot ornamented with scenes of the four seasons. Drawing the carriage were six splendid chestnut horses with painted hoofs and white manes. In back and front were impeccably uniformed black coachmen.

Both Washingtons had relaxed into their roles. Martha Washington found life more comfortable, adjusting to the peculiar hustle and bustle of the city and to its raucous noise and strange energy, so different from Mount Vernon.

The limits placed on her activities had been lifted, and she moved more easily into the social scene. As the First Lady she charmed select society with her affability. "I am still determined to be cheerful and to be happy," she had written to Mrs. Warren back in December, "for I have also learned from experience that the greater part of our happiness or misery depends upon our dispositions, and not upon our circumstances."

And while Congress debated, and the social scene maintained its hectic pace, the president once again became severely ill. In May he was stricken with pneumonia. Congress responded with stunned silence when physicians pronounced him near death. Even his opponents were in tears at the thought of losing him, for no one could conceive of government without this magnetic figure at its head.

In the slow, painful recovery, the president had time to think about the two critical illnesses he had suffered within the year. A third such attack, he said, "more than probable will put me to sleep with my fathers."

On the advice of physicians he tried to invest less emotional energy on the controversial issues before Congress. And though he supported Alexander Hamilton in his proposals, he carefully avoided making his thoughts known except to an intimate few, lest he influence the debates. Basic to Washington's views was the separation of powers—that the executive branch of government must not abuse its authority, and should not interfere in legislative matters.

To show the public a lighter side of government, the Washingtons turned July 4, Independence Day, into a popular celebration. Hundreds of visitors were welcomed to the gardens of the president's house, where the Washingtons officiated at long tables set with wine and cake. Church bells rang out all day, and at night fireworks brightened the sky over the Hudson.

But the pressures of office continued. For weeks the president tried to deal with the problems of the American Indians. Policies had yet to be worked out on this most sensitive question, though the president made clear his opposition to the grabbing of Indian land. His ideas put him into conflict with land speculators who considered the whole of the country free to take and occupy.

The president was forceful on another issue—religion. His support for religious differences encouraged minorities such as Jews and Catholics, Quakers and Baptists, to build their own churches and synagogues. The Washingtons' regular church attendance also encouraged other denominations to flourish.

After passing the bill to assume payments of national and state debts, Congress finally adjourned on August 12. And the president, who considered travel part of official duty, took a trip to Rhode Island to welcome the belated entry of that state into the union. Before that he had visited Long Island, leaving behind him on the doors of inns plaques reading "The president slept here."

On his return from his travels on August 21, he helped Martha, the children, and the servants pack up the house. They were ready to leave New York for Mount Vernon before taking up their duties in Philadelphia. Always underestimating the esteem in which they were held, they thought they would quietly depart.

Except for a dinner the president gave for state and city officials, no elaborate plans had been made. But on August 30, a hot, sunny day, the streets near the president's house quietly filled with people. Many, feeling bereft, were in tears. At 10:30 A.M., the family, accompanied by government officials, left the residence. The crowd followed them down to the McComb Wharf on the Hudson, where they were to take the presidential barge to Paulus Hook.

Before embarking, the president turned, looked sadly at the

crowd of well-wishers, and said a few words, thanking them for their kindness during his stay in New York. A thirteen-gun salute from the Battery announced that the family was boarding the barge. As it was rowed away, once again the president turned, waved his hat, and said a single word, "Farewell." He would never return to New York City.

For many years people would talk about the time that the Washingtons lived among them, giving a boost to a war-torn city. They had helped make it a commercial, political, and social center of the country, and it would never lose that leading position.

The president had been diligent about gracing the city's institutions. He had a box at the theater; he attended commencement exercises at Columbia College; and he was present at the celebration at the rebuilding of Trinity Church, where a canopied pew had been set aside for him and the family.

The city the Washingtons left behind on August 30, 1790, was a polyglot of religions and languages. Right after the war, immigrants of different ethnic stock began arriving at the port of New York at the rate of three thousand a year. The city's piers and docks resounded not only with the noise of new arrivals but with the turmoil of a booming foreign trade. New York would continue to build, tear down, and rebuild—just as it had when the Washingtons came to town.

PLACES TO VISIT

You can still find reminders of the old seaport town in the southernmost tip of Manhattan. Narrow winding streets, historic buildings, and old churches contrast with the towering skyscrapers that now line the streets.

If you search along the East River, you will discover a fragment of Cherry Street. The neighborhood where the Washingtons lived has been swallowed up by a huge housing complex and the steel girders of the Brooklyn Bridge. But down on the East River, near the bridge, is Peck Slip, where Martha Washington disembarked from the presidential barge in May 1789 to take up her duties as First Lady.

Only a tablet on the building at 39 Broadway designates the site of the second presidential mansion where the Washingtons lived from February 23 to August 30, 1790.

At the tip of Manhattan is Battery Park. Some two hundred years ago, before it was extended and reshaped by landfill to its present proportions, the president walked along this promenade and looked out over the sea to the many sailing ships that carried on the nation's trade.

Fraunces Tavern still stands at Broad and Pearl streets. The upstairs long room has a low ceiling and floors made of broad wooden planks and is furnished with Federal antiques. On the walls are engravings and other reminders of the historic moment in 1783 when George Washington bade farewell to the officers of the Revolutionary Army. The tavern is now one of five historic structures that comprise Fraunces Tavern Museum.

Though the Federal Hall Memorial stands at Broad and Wall streets, it is not the old Federal Hall of Washington's inaugural. You will search in vain there for the balcony on which Washington took his oath of office. Outside the present handsome building is J.Q.A. Ward's statue of Washington, erected in 1883. Plans are under way to create a Museum of American Constitutional Government in Federal Hall, with an exhibit about the Federal Hall of 1789.

Trinity Church still makes its presence felt in the crowded neighborhood of present-day Wall Street and Broadway. On view is the pew that was set aside for the Washington family. In the churchyard can be found the gravesite of Alexander Hamilton.

Finally there is St. Paul's Chapel, a handsome Georgian building that dates back to 1766. Standing on its old site of Broadway and present-day Fulton Street, it is a repository of historic events. Washington walked to St. Paul's after his inauguration, and it was here that the family worshiped while Trinity was undergoing one of its many renovations.

The gravestones in the burial grounds of both St. Paul's and Trinity are unique relics of the time two hundred years ago when New York was the site of revolutionary struggles and when church steeples dominated the skyline.

On the streets now occupied by City Hall and City Hall Park once stood the Bridewell, the Almshouse, and the debtors' prison. These old buildings have been removed from the landscape and only in books can one find their stories.

FURTHER READING

The library is the best place for further studies of George and Martha Washington and their historic stay in New York. I did most of the research for this book at the library of The New-York Historical Society, where a helpful staff made materials available. Maps and newspapers of the period were especially valuable in helping me visualize the era.

I read many books and I list here a few of those that were useful to me.

I. N. P. Stokes's *The Iconography of Manhattan Island* (New York: Robert H. Dodd, 1915–1928) is a rich resource for detailed descriptions of daily events.

Among the countless books on George Washington are the definitive four-volume biography by James Thomas Flexner (Boston: Little, Brown, 1965–1972) and the single volume distilled from the larger work, called *Washington, the Indispensable Man* (Boston: Little, Brown, 1974).

Among the many books on the inauguration is T. E. V. Smith's *The City of New York in the year of Washington's inauguration, 1789* (New York: Anson D. F. Randolph and Co., 1889).

The books on Martha Washington have not been updated. Among the biographies I read are Elswyth Thane's *Washington's Lady* (New York: Dodd, Mead, 1960) and Alice Desmond's *Martha Washington, our first lady* (New York: Dodd, Mead, 1942).

Important to my research were the letters of Abigail Adams (Boston: Wilkes Carter, 1848) and *New Letters of Abigail Adams, 1788–1801* (Boston: Houghton Mifflin, 1947).

A fine book on the Constitution is Richard B. Bernstein and Kym Rice's *Are We To Be a Nation? The Making of the Constitution* (Cambridge: Harvard University Press, 1987).

To learn more about the city, there is Raymond A. Mohl's *Poverty in New York, 1783–1825* (New York: Oxford University Press, 1971) and Edgar J. McManus's *A History of Negro Slavery in New York* (Syracuse, NY: Syracuse University Press, 1966).

For young readers I would like to suggest the following titles.

Brick, John. *They Fought for New York*. New York: G. P. Putnam's Sons, 1965.

Cavallo, Diana, with photographs by Leo Stashin. *The Lower East Side: A Portrait in Time*. New York: Macmillan, 1971.

Davis, Burke. *Black Heroes of the American Revolution*. New York: Harcourt Brace Jovanovich, 1976.

De Pauw, Linda Grant. *Founding Mothers: Women in America in the Revolutionary Era*. Boston: Houghton Mifflin, 1975.

Jackson, Florence and J. B. *The Black Man in America, 1619–1790*. New York: Franklin Watts, 1970.

Meltzer, Milton. *George Washington and the Birth of Our Nation*. New York: Franklin Watts, 1986.

Siegel, Beatrice. *Sam Ellis's Island*. New York: Four Winds Press-Macmillan, 1985.

I N D E X